ADVANCE PRAISE

"More than just survival, Charity has created a new way of being for herself and her children. *The Widow's Survival Guide* will be a welcome tool to others to help them do the same. With wisdom that comes from experience and with humor and humility, Charity offers hope and practical steps through the darkness and difficulty of grief into the light and new possibilities of life. For those who have experienced grief and loss especially, but for anyone who wants to understand more about the way of grief, this book is a welcome companion on the journey."

–The Reverend Tracy Fye Weatherhogg

"Through this book, Charity Hyams will take your hand to both guide and reassure, utilizing just the right mix of practicality and existentialism. She anticipates and normalizes the complex emotions associated with early widowhood. I will recommend this book to my patients and friends."

—Megan Greenleaf, M.D.

"As a clinical social worker, a large part of my work is experiencing empathy with my clients. Reading this book gave such great insight into the raw feelings, thoughts, and experiences of a grieving widow and parent. I highly recommend other clinicians read this book to help inform your work with someone who is grieving. Thanks Charity for inviting us into your life and sharing your beautiful words."

—Heather Hildebrant, LICSW

"Charity brings you into her new world as a young widow with three small boys with a raw emotional pull. Her honest portrayal of loss is amazing. The helpful suggestions are for anyone going through a loss of a loved one."

—Irma Wesphal, widow and loss of a son

"*The Widow's Survivor Guide* is much more than a book. It is an act of kindness, a shower of healing nectar, a salve for the wound of grief. Sure to become a classic, this beautifully written guide is at once heartbreaking and heartwarming. A brave and deeply human account of embracing unbearable loss, Charity's hard won "brokenly beautiful" elixir is powerful medicine for anyone suffering loss."

–Robin Winn, LMFT

"*The Widow's Survival Guide* is a heartbreaking journey of myriad emotions, love, and loss. I found myself holding my breath through some of the painfully practical details and advice to widows. The love expressed in this book is tangible, honest and devastating."

–Ana-Maria Figueredo, author of *The Secret Art of Selling Insurance*

"*The Widow's Survivor Guide* is a quick glimpse into the painful hours, days, and months after losing a life partner, while still having to answer to the call, "Mom." This raw and real recount will give pause, yet reassure those who find themselves in this sad situation that they are not alone. Grief is messy. Charity's story will help readers count their blessings. A necessary read for both widows and those in their close circles trying to bolster, grieve, and understand all at once."

–LJ Coppola, MBA and Death Coordinator

"Being a widow, I experienced so much confusion because I felt things that were not understood by people who had never through my journey.

This book acknowledged and validated my feelings. For instance, the widow brain or how I was exhausted all the time.

I also had similar concerns that I would mess up my child because I was often sad.

The journey into widowhood while being a mother will be much easier with guidance such as this book and I am forever grateful for Charity's generosity and bravery to share her story. She inspires me to share mine."

–Sri Purna Widari, widow with small children

"Charity has fully entered into her grief journey with open eyes, an open heart, and great courage. Journaling and sharing her story through Facebook has helped her engage her grief and helped all of us understand and support her. She has found her way to balance the grieving and the moving into her new reality. Her writing is heart-warming and touching because it is so clear and honest. A grieving mother will find solace in these words, perhaps relief that she is not alone or crazy, encouragement that it does get better, and an invitation to enter fully into the grief (it will not swallow you completely) and not push it away (that never works). I would also recommend it for relatives and friends of a grieving mother (or father!), so they can better understand what it's like and join her in her journey. As a professional social worker working with parents who have experienced fetal or infant death, Charity's openness to her grief and to sharing it has expanded my knowledge of the grief process, making me a better resource for my clients."

–Cynthia Heinrich, social worker

"Charity is an inspiring and tender voice in the landscape of loss and grief. I feel fortunate to have discovered her work, and sense that an ally is supporting me from afar. Her story and spirit is shared in that manner, and I wish others to receive this gift."

–Allison Behrstock, widow and educator

THE WIDOW'S SURVIVAL GUIDE

THE WIDOW'S SURVIVAL GUIDE

Living with Children After the Death of Your Spouse

CHARITY PIMENTEL-HYAMS

NEW YORK

LONDON • NASHVILLE • MELBOURNE • VANCOUVER

The Widow's Survival Guide

Living with Children After the Death of Your Spouse

Published in New York, New York, by Morgan James Publishing in partnership with Difference Press. Morgan James is a trademark of Morgan James, LLC. www.MorganJamesPublishing.com

ISBN 9781631950209 paperback
ISBN 9781631950216 eBook
Library of Congress Control Number: 2020931936

Cover Design Concept:
Jennifer Stimson

Cover & Interior Design by:
Christopher Kirk
www.GFSstudio.com

Editor:
Bethany David

Book Coaching:
The Author Incubator

Author Photo:
Jami Zmurko

Morgan James is a proud partner of Habitat for Humanity Peninsula and Greater Williamsburg. Partners in building since 2006.

Get involved today! Visit
MorganJamesPublishing.com/giving-back

If our loved ones are like candles that only are snuffed when the last thought of them has been thought, we intensify their flame. I will not hide it under a bushel, no! I'm going to let it shine! When the time comes and I am wherever we go, or don't go. ... Let someone love me this much. Let someone write to me and about me. Let me become poems and psalms and words and stories; such beautiful stories. Words never die. They lie dormant until eyes soften to them, and alive as the moment they were written, they return. Let us all be reborn through our words.

TABLE OF CONTENTS

Chapter 1:

I Wish You Were Not Reading This Book

Dear Friend,

Who knows, as you're reading this, it could have been months after your other half has died, or it could have been days. Your children are being more difficult, and you are exhausted to the bone. You realize you didn't know what the expression "bone tired" meant until now. Your mind is tired, your body is tired, you don't want to think, but you dread forgetting. Maybe your spouse battled cancer for years, or possibly you sent him or her off to work and they never returned. You could have watched it all happen, helpless to save the one you loved, or you could never have even gotten to say goodbye.

This is what I do know: you have children, infants to preschoolers. You were a mother and a wife and now you are a solo parent who is deeply in grief—and grief, my friend, is a tsunami.

Let's go through any day in the first year together. You wake up, turn over, and are actually shocked for the hundredth time that your spouse is not there. When you do realize once more that your life just got ripped out from under you, you might have the strong urge to not get up at all or even not want to be alive. Your three-year-old comes in and jumps on your face, and you take him downstairs to feed him and get him dressed and ready for school. Then you wash-rinse-repeat with the two other children. You do this with bricks around your ankles and on your shoulders. Cereal feels hard. Milk feels impossible. Spoons—oh, eff the spoons.

Somehow you get every single one of your children into the car. They are twenty minutes late for school because of the fight about boots that do not fit anymore. You drop the older children off, and you still have the one-year-old. Great! Let's go to the doctor's with the one-year-old. Who doesn't love pap smears holding a child in your arms? Next, you travel to the lawyer's to sign more papers, and then you get to pick up your preschooler from half-day preschool. All the while, what is running through your head is, *Should I sell the house? Is my five-year-old dealing with this well? God, I miss my husband. Should I go on medication? I am not sleeping, but I can't take anything that will knock me out in case of an emergency. I am so unbelievably tired.*

You go back to when it was good, to when you had a spouse who could take off work so that you could have an appointment by yourself. You remember being held, and loved, and kissed. You remember falling asleep and waking up next to the one you chose for life. *For life,* none of this dying while our kid is still in flipping diapers!

And then, in the middle of the kitchen floor, you cry. You ugly cry. Your three-year-old asks you what is wrong. You say you miss Daddy. Loneliness, crushing, heavy loneliness covers you and breathing becomes hard.

Oh, but look at the time—you have got to pick up your five-year-old from school. You get to the school and get a gentle reminder to bring a hat and socks tomorrow. Screw hats and screw socks, your husband is dead. Oh, wait. You have no food. Honestly, you can't even make a list because your brain hurts. You go to the grocery store and are one step away from a panic attack. When you leave you don't have what you need and you have a whole bunch of things you don't want. You are so tired the kids get peanut butter for dinner and put in front of the TV until bedtime. Bedtime is a lot of yelling and stomping and crying. You get them in bed and just want to go to bed too, but when you get there, you can't fall asleep. So you get in the shower and cry some more. When you do finally nod off, you get three to four and a half hours of rest before you do it all again.

This is not life. This is not what you want for yourself or your children. You are living in a never-ending tornado of grief and helplessness and you are getting pulled into a dangerous routine. If you stay in this cycle, it will eventually lead to paralysis. You can't move forward, you can't stay still. It all hurts, and you cannot imagine a day when you will smile willingly.

There is another way, a way that makes things a little lighter, a little more bearable. There is a way where the future, although never ever again what you hoped it would be, looks worth living. I want the waves of grief to not pull you under but teach you the lessons of love and loss. I want to open your heart and eyes to the possibility of beauty and peace in the midst of turbulence and the ever-present grief. I want you to feel supported in your journey and feel the presence of someone who was there before you. I want you to see that widows do make it to a new normal. I want to teach you that way. Because I know you can do this. I am here to help you.

Chapter 2:

MY PERSONAL NIGHTMARE
AND THE ROAD OUT

Hi, my name is Charity, and I am thirty-eight as I write this book. I was thirty-seven when Ollie, my husband of twelve years (we'd been together fourteen), took his last breath on this earth. At the time, we had three boys, ages five, three, and one.

Ollie worked as an IT manager, which had taken us to Vermont just twelve months prior, though all of our family was in Cincinnati. On the morning of May 3,

2018, we were getting ready to visit Ohio. Ollie's father, Rick, was in the hospital with cholangiocarcinoma cancer that had metastasized, and according to Ollie's brother, he was going downhill quickly. Our van had thrown a belt, and Ollie had ordered the parts from the manufacturer. Ollie was handy with cars and often did repairs. While Ollie went to get the parts and tools, I dropped our older two at school and had a babysitter take the baby, Louis, to Walmart to get socks so I could pack.

When I returned to the house, Ollie had the van taken apart in our driveway. He asked me to be the above-the-car lever puller as he adjusted the belt underneath. He straightened everything and said, "Okay, push the lever." I can still hear the creak of the van as the jack slipped. I can remember it distinctly. I can hear Ollie's cry of agony and him telling me to get the jack lever from the bag. I got the lever and cranked the jack back down and then cranked the jack back up. I remember telling him, "Just hold on, baby." I remember telling him I was working on it. I remember the blood trickling from Ollie's nose and mouth.

While working on the jack, I called 911 from my cell phone. By the time the first policeman got there, I had gotten the jack far enough up that the minivan was off

Ollie's chest but not high enough to drag him out. The police officer tried to help lift the front of the van and then the jack fell again. With both of us lifting, we dragged the car off of Ollie. I remember that another police officer had shown up and they were discussing whether or not CPR was appropriate, because Ollie was still breathing. I am amazed at how hard Ollie fought to stay alive.

One officer tried to keep me busy until the ambulance took Ollie to the hospital. I try not to have regrets, but I do not think I ever touched Ollie in those final moments. I did not get to say, "I love you." I wish I had. The ambulance was in my driveway for a very long time. The police officer asked if I had anyone who could take me to the hospital, and so, after I called twice, my friend Laura came and picked me up. When we got to the hospital, we were taken directly to "the room," the smaller family waiting room, reserved for private doctor-family conversations.

I said to Laura, "He's dead."

She said, "We don't know that."

We sat in the little room. Several social workers came in and out of the room to check on us and let us know that we would be receiving additional information shortly. After what felt like forever, the doctor (who coincidentally I had met a week before at a baby shower) got to give me the news that the injuries were far too invasive and that Ollie was dead. The love of my life, the father of my children, the keeper of all my stories and my partner in life was gone. Poof. He was healthy and alive in the morning and dead before noon. I went and saw him. I called family. I cried. And then I realized I had no idea what to do next.

Laura (whom I lovingly and gratefully called my death coordinator) took over and got my middle child picked up from school, called the funeral home, helped me ask questions of and answer questions from the detective on the case, and figured out who needed to know what, when, and why. I remember the team of social workers at the hospital talking at me, though I have no recollection of what they said.

In an hour and a half at the most, my whole life had changed and gone into the crapper. I was no longer a married stay-at-home mom of three boys. I was a solo parent who had no idea what kind of money I had, what I was going to do, or if I would have to uproot my family. I knew nothing.

In the next weeks, Laura and I worked on logistics, like funerals, social security, and life insurance. All the while, I was raising three boys who were still in definite need of raising.

As all of that slowed down, I realized that my husband, who had kept the same wedding picture on his phone screen since smartphones came out, who made dinner every night and put the kids to bed, who shared one plate with me at every meal, who would look at pictures of our kids after they went to bed, was dead. Dead. Not coming back. Not ever. Not even for a moment.

At times like these, your brain is so deep into processing that there are moments you are pretty sure that your situation is all made up. I kept thinking about string theory and praying I would wake up on a different timeline, one where Ollie was in bed next to me. Just let me wake up on a different timeline.

Very early on, *you* have to make the choice to live. You have to make the choice that you are going to move forward. In the beginning, I made this choice because I had decided that I could not make my children's lives harder. Later it was because I believe that I am here for a reason.

I am a researcher at heart and read many, many books on grief. Some I loved but the one thing that kept coming up missing is that when you have small children, you don't have time to traditionally mourn. I would have loved to have spent a month in bed, not changing my sheets, smelling Ollie until there was not even a whiff of him left, but I could not. I could not stop my daily activities, and I could not even stop social events if I wanted to create a semblance of normalcy with my children. I got creative and I developed ways to process while living.

I still had diapers, and preschool, and bedtimes. How do I go from not wanting to wake up to finding a new life? It was not the life I planned or wanted, but one that was worth living. That, my friend, is what this book is. It is also my testament of love to my beautiful husband. I am now a year and a half out. I laugh, I cry, I dance. I opened an Airbnb. I have birthed this book and my widow coaching business. I have traveled with my children to Florida, Maine, Ohio, Virginia, North Carolina, New Hampshire, Kentucky, and New York. I have traveled with friends or by myself to Montreal; Lake George, New York; Woodstock, Vermont; Washington, DC; Toronto; and Jamaica. I have picked up the joy of photography. I have lived. I have spread some of Ollie's ashes throughout many of these places, and even when I did not take him to a place physically, he's always been with me. My whole philosophy on life and love has morphed into a love song for what has gone and what I still have. I worry less and love more. I focus on love. I cling to what is good and I discard the rest. Throughout this book, I give you processes and tips and actions to take to help incorporate your grief. Grief never goes away, but it becomes a part of you. Throughout the book, you will see my journal entries from the first year in italics. I have been where you are, and it is *hard*. Let me be the hand you hold when you need advice.

At your funeral, they spoke of your self-confidence and your unquestioning stance of right and wrong. They spoke of your defense of the weak in the face of the bullies that threatened and your compassion for others. They spoke of your wisdom in all things. They spoke of your musicality and wit. They spoke of how you made them feel about themselves.

I stood and listened and thought all that and more.

Your heart was so big and so open; I saw it broken because your giant exterior fooled others. I saw you face little men who thought they were giants. I saw you hold babies like precious cargo in one giant hand. I saw your mind whirl and process giant problems until you could break them into small parts and move through them to find a solution. I saw your heart open to misfits, to children, and to me.

Your laugh was what I aimed for every day. Your guidance was spot on. Your love was fierce and encompassing. You noticed everything and everyone. You remembered and that made people feel heard and seen. Your stories and wit were legendary. Your hugs were home.

Your shoes were ridiculously large and impossible to fill.

Chapter 3:

WHAT DOES THE PROCESS LOOK LIKE?

I n creating this book, I took all of the pieces that helped me the most, split them into categories, and created this love letter to you and to Ollie. Each part of the process is equally as important as the last. To make a whole, each part needs to be addressed, cared for, and respected. I have ordered the steps to each build on the last. I have also purposely made this book short so that if you can't make it through a lot of words, you can easily get to what you can use. Grief is a constant. This is work I did to incorporate grief into my life. Grief can be a tool to focus on what is important and remove from our lives what is not. It is choosing the road that leads to purpose and life while holding on to the core of who you will forever love. Let them move you forward, not hold you back.

Step 1: First things first. Immediate things to do or delegate after your spouse has died. In death, there are things that absolutely have to get done. From burial to social security, this is what I know you will have to deal with in the first couple of weeks. Even if you are past those weeks, check through and see if there is anything you missed.

Step 2: What to expect in grief. Realize you are not crazy; you are grieving. There are many symptoms of grief. There are things you might not expect. All of these things are normal and I want you to feel that you are not alone and you are not in any way crazy.

Step 3: Support yourself in daily living. Steps to support yourself in getting through the day, every day. These are the foundation blocks to build on for a healthier grief journey.

Step 4: Find your tribe. Creating a support system for your needs physically, emotionally, and spiritually is key to a healthier grief process. Support is crucial in this timeframe. You will need your tribes to hold you up when you cannot do it yourself.

Step 5: Your children in grief. How to navigate being a solo parent with young children. This gives you practical advice on how to support your children in their own grief journey while they cope with the loss of a parent.

Step 6: Opening your heart again. Opening to love and joy when grief is so strong. Seeing through the cloud of grief is what gives us hope and purpose before we can develop those on a larger scale.

Step 7: Connecting to spirit. Reaching inside yourself to find wholeness. Realizing we are connected and loved in the midst of the loss of the physical.

Your children are worth this work. You are worth this work.

Chapter 4:

STEP 1 - FIRST THINGS FIRST

I hate to be the one to tell you, but you have no time in the first couple of weeks to process. Shock is your friend because you have a list that society gives you to do. Oh, and by the way, you still have children and they still *are* children.

If you were lucky enough to fall upon or be given this book, here is my checklist for what needs to get done. If it was up to me, I would just hold you and let you cry.

In the Hospital

In the hospital when you see your spouse, spend as much time as you want with him or her. If you want some of his or her hair, have someone bring you scissors. If you want pictures, take them. If you need a moment alone, ask for it.

If you feel like you need to do something, take the time and do it. My mother-in-law needed to take pictures and to watch her husband be cremated. When Ollie died, I sat with him, I touched his face, I hugged him, I held his hands, I kissed his mouth, I felt his chest hair, and I even groped him because I thought he would have appreciated the goodbye. I told him how much I loved him, I told him that he was irreplaceable, I told him that my love will go on and that I would do my best to help our children remember him. I told him I was sorry I didn't save him. I told him I was so sorry.

Take your time. If you decide to cremate, this is your last time together. Cherish it.

I know that for some of you, there will be no remains to visit or the remains will be gruesome and not who you knew. For you, my heart hurts for your loss of closure. What I would say to you is do whatever you feel like you need to do. My friend Elizabeth lost her husband, James, in such a way that the remains could not be recovered. She tells her children,

Their remains are not where they are. The one you love is in the wind, and the rain; the sunshine and the storms. They are in the music that pulls at your heart and takes your breath away or lets you breathe deeper. They are in you. When you love someone they become a part of you. That will always be.

We have a headstone. It is near James's parents' headstones. We find James in the songs that play on the radio or in the buds of the trees or the bodies of water.

We take James with us everywhere. We have picnics, and we bring his picture. We take his boots and a set of clothes if we ever go anywhere even just for a night.

So I guess we find our own ways to carry him.

I wish I had known this. Oscar, my oldest, still wants to see his dad dead. We took pictures and I showed them to Oscar, but there is a lot of research that shows that children better process the idea of death and endings and saying goodbye if they get to physically see their parent after they have died. Children are so resilient and beautiful that they do not have preconceived notions of what death is. I urge you to ask your children if they want to see their parent. Closure is a big deal. Try not to put your perception of what it would look or be like for them. I wish I had given Oscar that choice.

When you are in the hospital, they will ask you whom you plan to use as your funeral home within twenty minutes of initially informing you that you need one. If you have a church family, or someone who has done this whole death thing recently, call and ask about their experience with a funeral home. You will be spending time with the funeral home, so you want to like them and you want a smooth experience.

If your spouse's death was an accident or if you have been injured in any way, you need to get your physical needs met. Get checked out. You are critical to your children's health and well-being; take care of you. I wrenched my back trying to pull the minivan. My foot is still numb eighteen months later. I had two X-rays to ensure nothing was broken—but there are still physical residual reminders.

Telling Friends and Family

By this time, you now need to let important people know that your spouse has died. I felt the need to do this myself for close relatives and friends and Ollie's employer. For everyone else, I created a caringbridge.org page so that I could keep my whole circle in the know without repeating myself. I updated that page and then put the link on Facebook so that there was a specific public place to interact with everyone. Ollie's accident was also in a blurb in our local paper.

The Funeral Home and Service

With the funeral home, you will have to decide if you are going to bury or cremate, if you are going to have a viewing or a closed casket, what casket, where the casket is going, and so on. They will also help you with placing the obituary and the pre-obituary, which state the time and place of the service. This is also the place that will produce your death certificates. Get at least five to ten death certificates. There are places that will only accept an original, official copy. With Ollie, because his death was an accident, they sent him from the hospital to the medical examiner's office for an autopsy. There was a routine investigation done by the police. In this kind of case, the death certificate can take longer. They will offer the option of a memorial service.

You will have to decide if, where, and when you are going to do a service. If you are associated with a church, synagogue, mosque, or temple, you will coordinate with them. Even if you are not affiliated, many times it's still possible to coordinate with them, usually for a fee. If this doesn't appeal to you, the other option is the funeral home or a separate location. This can be handed over to someone else or you could oversee everything. My advice on this is that you do you. Focus on what feels important. If something feels extraneous, let someone else do it or don't do it at all. If you feel like letting others be included, that is fine. If you don't, don't. When Ollie died, Laura and I planned a family-friendly service where the pastor read the children's book *Invisible String* by Patrice Karst. It is about an invisible string of love that can never be broken, not by distance or death, and connects us all. I gave Ollie's eulogy because he was mine, and I could not let anyone else do that. My cousins performed "Georgica Pond" by Johnnyswim, and there was an ice cream truck. We had to hold services twice, once in Vermont and once in Cincinnati. We had photographers at both so that my children would know who loved their Daddo.

Do what feels right to you. Private or public, say goodbye in your way.

Paperwork and Benefits

Your children are entitled to social security death benefits if your spouse has paid into social security. If you are a stay-at-home mom or meet certain income requirements you may be entitled to benefits as well. File for this as quickly as possible. First, you can call your regional SSA office and go through an initial interview, and then they will set an appointment for you. The appointment is usually scheduled a month and a half out. It's often also possible to sit and wait in the office and see if an appointment slot opens up unexpectedly. That is the option I chose.

You do need the death certificate for this step. What you get per month as a spouse is based on the earnings your spouse put into the social security system through the years. Your surviving children are eligible until they graduate from high school or turn eighteen.

If you or your spouse are military, check with your branch for entitlements that you have through your branch of service. Some of the added entitlements are bereavement camps and counseling.

If you have life insurance, you will have to contact the policyholder with the death certificate. If this is through an employer, you will be going through the company your spouse worked for. If the payout is a large sum of money, get a trusted financial advisor, someone who will look at the long-term and be very mindful and conservative with your money. You will want to make a budget and set long-term plans.

You will also need a lawyer to draw up a new will for you and deal with any probate laws that may be applicable in your state. Each state is different, so you will have to talk to a lawyer to find out information pertaining to you. Most lawyers ask you to sign a letter of intent for their services and leave a retaining fee.

You will have to call and cancel any open accounts for your spouse. This includes credit cards, student loans, phones, retirement accounts, and any utility that is in their name. Most if not all of these will require a death certificate. It took me fourteen months and a friend holding my hand to cancel Ollie's cellphone line. All of this can be harder than you would think it should be.

Childcare

Set up childcare for all of your children. You will need time. There should be plenty of people asking what they can do at this early stage. Ask them to take your children and do things with them. You can split them individually or as a group, but you will need all the help you can get. Set people up to make your children's lunches and transport your kids to and from school. When people ask, give them tasks to make your life easier. I always appreciated when people took my children and did things that made the children feel normal, because I was not normal. Swinging by classmates' birthday parties at the play gym is not going to be fun during this timeframe.

Things to Leave for Later

If you can, save big decisions like putting the house on the market, relocating, or jumping into another relationship for later, after you are out of shock and are more aligned with yourself.

Most Importantly

My friend, most importantly, feel your grief. It's necessary to feel it with whomever you are with and wherever you are. I have cried in grocery stores, in my driveway, in the car while parked, in the shower, on the floor with my children. Feel it when it comes. Be a conduit. Let it in and let it flow out. Don't keep it. Feel it. Your spouse was worth the grief. Grief is love. Talk about them. Say their name. Own them. They are yours forever.

Chapter 5:

STEP 2 - WHAT TO EXPECT IN GRIEF

When you are in grief and, in the beginning, shock, there are physical, emotional, and spiritual symptoms. I have personal experience with all of the symptoms I will list. This list is, I am sure, in no way exhaustive. I am going to list them first and then touch on them. Know that you are normal and that grief can be doggedly unyielding.

Things you can experience in grief include

- widow brain
- PTSD
- eating issues
- exhaustion
- sleep issues
- inability to read
- anger
- extreme anxiety
- loss of friendships
- physical pain
- thoughts of wanting to be dead

Know that all of these are normal. Know that you are not crazy. Know that this is not an exhaustive list. I am telling you that you are normal, normal for grief. I am telling you that grief is the reason for all of this. I am telling you because I needed to be told.

Widow Brain

In May 2018 when Ollie died, I had a five-year-old, a three-year-old, and a one-year-old, so I was intimately familiar with "mommy brain." With the children so close together in age, I never left mommy brain. I would take the wrong turns for places I had gone every week for a year. I would leave my purse on the top of the car. What I would never have guessed is that there is a worse brain: widow brain.

Widow brain can be bad enough that you seek medical help because you feel like you are going crazy. You are not. You are grieving, and grieving takes up brain space.

Widow brain for me meant losing the keys to my rental car almost every day. It meant needing people to repeat what was said over and over, having a lot of trouble filling out paperwork, and generally feeling unmoored and unbalanced. This for me is a long-term symptom. I am now fourteen months out and while some symptoms have lessened for me over time, they can and will return.

Things that have been helpful for me in dealing with widow brain are lists, asking close, trusted friends to remind me of things, and respecting the days that are really hard and not doing much "brain work" on those days. I call those days or weeks the "I am having trouble adulting days." These days, I have an inability to make decisions or complete tasks. I try to be very gentle with myself on these days. I have been late on paying bills, not because I did not have the money or have forgotten, but could not get myself to sit down and press send on the computer. What can I say? This crap is a joy ride.

PTSD

Post-traumatic stress disorder (PTSD) is very common in the widow community, both in widows who experience taking care of their loved one and widows who lose their loved one quickly and unexpectedly. PTSD is an emotional reexperiencing of the trauma of death many months later. PTSD can be all-consuming and take you back to a moment in time that overwhelms current reality and places you back in that space and time when you first faced the loss of your loved one. Marissa puts her keys on a clip and tracking devices on important items so that when her increased startle response happens she does not lose or misplace items. She also had to discontinue use of glass cups, as so many broke when she was startled. Marissa uses a meditation app three times a day along with CBD to manage symptoms.

There are therapeutic treatments for PTSD such as eye movement desensitization and reprocessing

(EMDR), trauma sensitive yoga, breathwork, and neurofeedback. All of these help alleviate symptoms of trauma. Out of the list of experiences above, PTSD is the one for which seeking a supportive psychological medical team is advised.

Eating Issues

Ollie died in May and the children missed quite a bit of their last couple weeks of school for funerals and other death-related travel. When I started the new school year, I walked into the building with my three-year-old, and the director looked at me and said, "Wow, you look great. You have lost a ton of weight." I looked at her and said, "Yeah I call it the death diet" and went on my way. For almost a month after Ollie died, I did not feel I could eat. I don't know what part was worse: the chewing, the smell, the taste, the feeling when food hit my stomach, or how it came out. The irony at this time was the meal trains. We would get a new huge meal every couple days and the smell alone made me want to gag. Juiced fruit or soup felt okay sometimes, so that is what I did. If anything felt okay to eat, I ate it right then.

The "death diet" is also something that has stayed with me. I eat irregularly and my body does not process food like it used to. Grief and stress are wicked good at messing with your digestive system. You, my friend, might have a different death diet, like wanting to eat everything you can find, or only wanting to eat ice cream, or, or, or. All of this is normal.

"You look so good." "Thanks it's the death diet." "Wow, that's dark." "Is it?"

"Being thinner will serve you well in the future." "I would rather be fat and happy."

I am not losing weight to become some better version of myself. My body does not like eating anymore. It is a visceral displeasure that ends in stomachaches, diarrhea, acid reflux, and just feeling awful. My body has physically rejected Ollie's death, as my heart has told it to do.

When you tell me I look good, I want to show you a picture of a rotting fruit, perfect on the outside but decayed and noxious on the inside. It is sick and barely holding the structure of the whole together. One small poke and it implodes.

I am not strong. I am not brave. The strong and the brave go into things they do not need to. I am putting one foot in front of the other, because I have no choice. I HAVE NO CHOICE. I live in a world that I do not want, but have no escape because my babies are still important. I will not throw more onto them than has already been heavily laid upon their shoulders to bear for the rest of their lives. I will not. I cannot. I am not brave. I am stuck because of love. I am stuck because I love.

Exhaustion

Sometimes I try to picture what grief would be like if I didn't have small children. What would I have done the first year after Ollie's death if there were no children to get me up and moving? I think for the first couple of months, I would have slept the entire day, every day, and stayed up all night. Exhaustion is *real*. Bone-cold, body-twitching, staring-into-corner exhaustion is a cold, hard truth of death. Your body and mind are processing loss all the time even when it is not conscious. It is exhausting.

Then you get to be a parent. Crap.

I have to be very careful now because I can fall asleep while driving. This was something that I never did before grief.

Sleep Issues

The not sleeping is the fun part. You are grieving, you can be exhausted, but that doesn't mean you will be able to sleep. Sleep issues are another symptom of grief. Want to sleep all the time? Normal. Want to sleep but can't for the life of you? Normal. I am the latter. In my case, I still have very little ability to meditate, so I am skipping that in my recommendations. If you can meditate, do it. Things that have helped me (sometimes) include playing a meditation or meditation-type music, avoiding phone and TV (though sometimes, if it is your brain thinking too much, some light television might help—you do you), reishi mushroom supplements, magnesium, CBD, essential oils, light massage, stretching/yoga, and, my favorite in this category, a weighted blanket.

Sleep is critical, especially with children. Seek medical intervention if needed. The hardest part with prescribed medication for me is finding the right balance of being able to wake up if the kids need me while falling asleep enough to stay asleep and be able to rise in the morning. You most likely will have to go through a couple of different medications and doses to find what works. I still use this choice as my last option. I always have something on hand. If I'm an hour and a half in and nothing else is working, then I use it.

In addition, in Vermont, where I live, marijuana is legal. I, for the first six months after losing Ollie, smoked an indica strain to get to sleep. It did not seem to keep me asleep but would relax me enough that I could fall asleep. Edibles actually worked best, but I had less access to them. If you are in a state where it is legal, a good sleep strain of marijuana might be a good choice.

Inability to Read

I am a voracious reader. I like books. I like the smell of them. I like the feel of them. I read around two books a week for most of my adult life. This is the symptom that surprised me the most. I sat down to read a document—I think it was at the funeral home—I would get through a page and have *absolutely no idea* what I had read. None. I did it again. *Nothing.* I was reading words. I knew I was reading words. But my comprehension was gone. I tried again with a book about grief (surprise, surprise). Same thing. Read a page, kept none of it. Since losing Ollie, I have trouble concentrating on the words, and I have trouble comprehending what I read when I do concentrate. So I mostly still do audiobooks.

Anger

I have days I wake up angry. Really angry. Like, "break dishes against the wall" angry. Like, "use every curse word known to man in the first fifteen minutes" angry. It could be directed at your spouse. I find I can be irrationally angry at drivers, at dishes, at my children. Be aware that even when you are feeling that you are angry because the toys are on the floor or your children are giving you a hard time at bedtime again, that the anger you feel is most likely misdirected.

I succeed at remembering this sometimes. Sometimes I don't. If it does come out directed at your spouse, allow yourself to feel it. It is okay to be pissed. Pissed that you are doing this all by yourself. Pissed that you are alone without your partner, pissed that life isn't what you signed up for. *Feel it*. Get a punching bag. Break something. Go scream in the backyard or shower. It's okay. I'm doing it with you. When you notice that you are yelling at your kids (they will turn out all right even if you yell), try to remember and get that anger out a different way.

Extreme Anxiety

Anger and extreme anxiety go hand and hand for me. In the first half year, I would not have admitted to anxiety. I did not put together what anxiety felt like in this situation. Now I know that when my child did something dangerous and I went off the handle, it was because I am so anxious when it comes to keeping my children, friends, and family safe that it comes out in anger. I also have experienced panic symptoms. I have trouble with large crowds, and there are weird things I cannot get myself to do. The most recent was when I signed the boys up for tee ball but could not get them to one practice. I even got them in the car on time for one of the practices and sat in the driver's seat sweating, my heart pounding, almost crying. I went and got pizza instead.

Breathing helps. Focus on your breath, closing your eyes if possible, and count your breaths. "Count of five in, count of five out" is an easy technique, as is circular breathing (in through your nose and out through your mouth). When I breathe, I focus on the sound, the sound of my breath in my head. I also have anxiety medication that I can take as needed. Regarding medication, I believe it is important to feel your grief, so I try to avoid medication that is taken constantly. This is a personal choice, so if you need more support, you do you. I do urge you to realize that grief is important and will not be denied. If you choose to medicate or self-medicate in a way that suppresses grief, it will be dealt with at some point. It does not go away.

Loss of Friendships

My close friends have changed. I have been lucky enough not to lose many friends, but the ranking of whom I call is very different. Some people do not understand grief. Some do not want to be around it. Some will disappear. Some will say and do things that are so hurtful you will want them to disappear. My favorite things I've been told so far have been:

- "Well the best part is your kids are so young they won't remember him."
- "You will find someone else" (said two days after Ollie died).
- "Didn't you just love what my card said?" (Um, since I don't remember my name half the time, sure.)
- From a very dear friend: "Where do you think Ollie is? If he did not accept Jesus Christ as his Lord and Savior, I guess he would be in hell."

My advice is that you keep who is supportive. You let

go of who is not. In the beginning, I did not own my truth enough to say what I felt I needed to after stupid comments; now I confront them—not in an angry way, but in a way that empowers me. If I went back, I would have said: "That is what breaks my heart the most. I dread that they might not remember anything of their incredible, loving, father." "I lost a person I cannot replace. I might find another husband, but I will never find another Ollie, and that is who I am grieving right now." I would have said, "Honestly, I have not opened my own mail for a month. I can't even read at the moment." To the last one, I should have said, "I feel very sad that your belief system would send such a wonderful man to such an awful place. For believing in a loving God, that does not feel loving at all." To all of my friends who have belief systems, again, you do you, but I wanted to share my story as authentically as possible.

My favorite line that I still say almost every day is when you get hit over and over again with, "How are you?" I answer plainly, "I'm here."

I have unpacked the burden of falsity. My words are truer. There is no hiding in platitudes. My face shows the depth of sorrow, joy, confusion, and love that my heart is feeling. Even my face has no filter anymore. My words are more to the point. There is no game left in me. This is me right now, honest and raw.

I know what is important in this life. I do not have to vacillate on inconveniences or small things. I have pinpoint focus on what is just extraneous stuff. My important is relationships. My important is three small boys with eyebrows and dimples like their Daddo. My important died under a minivan while the sky was blue and it was finally warming up after a long, long winter. My important is sharing compassion and joy. My important is seeing the divine spark in others. My important is laughing and loving.

It is freeing to cut all the clutter of life. I am more black-and-white in my truth. This is important. This is not. Ollie's death cut the tie to extraneous things. The clarity from loss is beautiful and terrifying. It all comes down to love. Love is hopefully our beginning and, if we are lucky, our end. I find the simplicity beautiful.

Physical Pain

In grief, I experience physical pain through my digestive system. My body does not process food in the same way it used to. You might have more headaches or back-aches—God, who knows what physically could come about, just because your body is working through the unthinkable. I also have not had feeling in half of my right foot since Ollie's death. My hamstrings, calves, and lower back are incredibly tight since the accident, and I have to be very conscious of stretching them so as not to have problems moving.

My grief became physical the day that Ollie died. I tried to pick up that van and in the end, he still died and with his death, I also lost the feeling in half of my right foot.

The physical presence of pain and loss, of death and dying is so close, like a lover. When my eyes are closed, I feel death immediately past my eyelashes. If I opened my eyes, death would be nose to nose with me. Staring me down.

And my foot is dead. How poetic. It is my right foot; the male side of the body in Eastern medicine. Dead.

When I forget for a second that death is staring back at me, I trip, or step on a Lego, and am brought back to reality, the reality that Ollie is dead. I close my eyes and feel death's breath once more.

Thoughts of Wanting to Be Dead

For the first eight months, one of my heart's greatest desires was to be with Ollie. What is important to hear about this one is that in no way was I suicidal. I just wanted to be with him. If you ever feel like you are making a plan or feel any action behind the idea of killing yourself, seek help immediately. *Now*. Right now. On very sad days, I always tell my inner circle. Always.

I also feel it is important to mention that when I am at the start of premenstrual symptoms, I can really feel much lower than normal. There have been many times that I have considered medication and then realized that my hormones were the last straw on the camel's back. I watch for this now, and, again, I tell my circle.

There is something I did not mention here. It is because grief is misdiagnosed as this quite often: depression. Grief is not depression and depression is not grief. You might suffer from depression, but it is separate. Grief is a process during which you will be sad. *For a reason*. In your case, a major reason.

Secondary Losses

Grief comes in the form of your primary loss and then secondary losses. Secondary losses are all of the things you lose on top of losing your spouse. They are things many people would not think of until they are in the situation. There is the loss of a co-parent, loss of income, loss of identity, loss of future dreams and goals. All of these are what you are internally and externally processing. Please be easy on yourself. Please. Please, please, my friend.

SECONDARY LOSSES

Chapter 6:

STEP 3 - FIND YOUR TRIBE

A t this time you could be in a room full of people who love you and feel utterly alone. Your partner, the one who shared all of your stories and knew you intimately, inside and out, is now gone. What the heck happened? In some ways this step will feel laborious and hard. It will feel like the exact opposite of what you want to do. If you are like me, I wanted to find a hole and crawl inside. I did not care about finding support for myself. Then, I would think of my babies. They do not deserve to lose both parents because I checked out.

They do not deserve the pain of a mom who was useless. So put your listening ears on. Get help. Find your tribe.

There are three tribes. You need them all. *You need them all.*

The first tribe is the home tribe. These are the day-to-day people who are going to keep you going. In the beginning, you will be overwhelmed with people who want to help. They will call, drop off food, and ask what you need. *I know this is not perfect or what you want.* You want to cry in the corner or sleep. Those darn babies and your love for them … *ask for what you need.* If you need to, write a list of the things you need and hand it out. Most people are not in any way intuitive. If you need people to mow your lawn, ask. If you need more child-care, ask. If you need people to drive the kids to school, ask. *Whatever* you need, ask. Ask until someone does it. Make the list. Ask. Ask. Ask.

My friend Laura was there from the beginning. I called her while the ambulance was still in the driveway. She came. She housed me; fed me; organized my funeral home, my lawyer, my financial adviser; she planned my memorial service and told me when to update my web-page. She was also the one who told me I would never have proper time to grieve. I had responsibilities and I would have to grieve around life.

I told my friend Lacey that mornings and evenings were the hardest. She showed up every morning. She heard every morning how much I missed Ollie. My friend Lyndsay went through every photo on my computer to make the slideshow for Ollie's funeral and looked through every box for Ollie's will. My friends Liz, Owen, and Cristy picked my children up for school and dropped them off again.

People like these are your physical help people. Most of them will disappear eventually back into their own busy lives, but they want to help now—and you should let them. Anything that takes the load from you is worth asking for. Even in later months, if you are struggling, ask.

Here is a list to start.

- Mow lawn
- Weed beds
- Do dishes
- Watch the kids
- Take the kids to parties
- Babysit the kids so you can doing something fun

- Fix the switch that won't turn on
- Do laundry, fold laundry, put away laundry
- Take the kids to school
- Make the kids lunches
- Make meals
- Change the beds
- Help put the kids to bed
- Help get the kids up
- Help purge
- Help go through your spouse's things
- Get mail
- Open mail
- Make important piles
- Clean house
- Clean car
- Grocery shop
- Rotate clothes seasons or sizes
- Organize appointments
- Take the kids to the dentist, therapy, or school functions
- Pay bills
- Errands
- Find or organize documents

The second tribe will not necessarily be who you think it should be. My second tribe was made up of some old friends but also many who were acquaintances at the time of Ollie's death. This tribe usually shows up and intuitively fills the roles that need to be filled.

I have about twelve friends and family in my inner circle. The Kvetching Order puts the most affected in the middle, then the circles go out by who is the next most affected and so on.

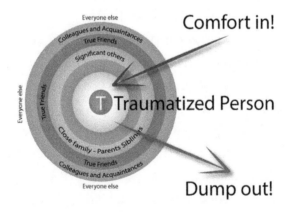

When you are looking for support, always turn to the less affected people. The biggest thing to grasp is that people who are closer to the loss will not be able to help you with yours. Look to people who have space to give support, and if that person needs support, they should look in a larger ring than themselves.

My inner circle is made up of my family and friends, not Ollie's family or my children, who are dealing with their own grief. This does not mean we are not supportive of each other's journeys. It means that people less affected have more room to support your journey. Some of my closest friends and my biggest supporters are the best things that came from Ollie's death and are the ones who field my pain and give comfort.

These are the people you call when you are on the floor and you don't know how to get up. These are the people who will answer the phone and listen to you say, "I just miss him." Most of the time these friends give no advice. They don't use platitudes. They sit with you in it. What I hear most is "I know." "I love you." "I wish that too." "This sucks."

Find the people who sit with you. Who let you cry. They hear your pain and don't try to change it. They just live it with you. They are the ones who come and get your kids, who fill in when you are too tired or gone to do what you need to do, who carry you when you can't do it yourself. They spend the anniversaries with you and invite you to holidays so you don't do them by yourself. They answer their phones day and night. They love you unconditionally. These are your gifts through grief. When you are in a better place, thank these few people who become your lifelines.

The other tribe is your grief tribe. If you are in a big city you might find a support group or club. I live in a small city in Vermont, so this tribe is mostly online and I go to Camp Widow, which is a widow conference that has break-out groups and a celebration where you can really connect to people who really get you. These are the people you will share your darkest, deepest moments with because they get it. They get the feeling of the half-life you are leading. They get the feeling of not wanting to be here. They get the feeling of being lost. I have about four groups on Facebook that I am active in. The nice thing is that online someone is always up. There is always someone available. Look for the groups that are totally supportive. These groups will open their hearts to your joys and concerns. If any group makes you feel less than or not accepted, it isn't your group. Leave and find a new one. My personal group is The Widow's Survival Guide.

You need people who, although their circumstances will never be identical, know grief intimately, have walked the journey themselves, or have walked it with others traveling the same journey. This is what I want to be for you.

Things to Note

Tell your tribe when you are struggling. Tell all of the tribes. Lay it out there. Do not hold on to it. Tell your tribe at home. Tell your tribe online. Tell your counselor. Tell them all. Sometimes you don't know where your help is going to come from, but you have to be vulnerable in order to receive that help. You have to be open to feel the love of others, and there is so much love for you.

It's okay to own your own truth and correct friends when they say something that feels off or wrong. I had plans to go away for Ollie's death day. I find it easier to do something different. My son was sick, so I canceled the plans. I texted one of my friends, and they replied with, "At least you will be too busy to think about it." This felt dismissive and completely wrong. There is nothing that I can do on Ollie's death day that will stop my thoughts of him. There is no hiding behind life. I choose what feels most supportive to do on the hard days for a reason. I wrote back and said, "No, I would not be too busy to think about it, I would just be thinking about it with vomit on my hands." I had a friend send me a gift that said, "God picks the prettiest flowers," and I asked if she thought I was ugly. Be honest with people. It saves a lot of misunderstanding and hurt. When I talk about my tribe, I am talking about people I love who love me. I try to say what I need to in a nonconfrontational way that I feel they can hear.

Some days you will be broken. Some days will be hard. These are the days that you will breathe and take one moment at a time—one moment at a time, one breath at a time. These days will feel like they go on forever. Know that tomorrow will most likely be better and if you have followed the advice above, your support system will surround you. Friend, know that I have been there, done that, and bought the t-shirt. Heck, I'm still doing these some days. I am still here. You will get through these. You are not alone. You are never alone.

Chapter 7:

STEP 4 - SUPPORT YOURSELF IN DAILY LIVING

aily living is something we cannot escape. If you didn't have children, maybe you could play the hermit card. But you do and, so, you can't. If you are reading this book you are looking for ways to take action to take some control back of your life. To feel in small ways that you are moving forward instead of standing still in grief. You are amazing. You really are. You getting out of bed is a feat of strength. I am so serious right now. I know you are doing it because you have to. I know that you do not want to and I know you are doing it anyway. Here are some of the ways I found to support myself in daily living.

Be selective on where your energy goes. I do not grocery shop. The grocery store is still one of my biggest triggers. I walked into the grocery store shortly after Ollie died and felt like I couldn't breathe. I felt panicky and sweaty. I did not know what I wanted or needed. I left the store, and the four things I went in to buy, I did not have when I walked out. So I have groceries delivered. Or do the "deliver to your car" thing. Triggers are events, things, or words that take us out of our thinking brain. Triggers are different for each of us, often taking us for surprise at first. If there is an activity that I know I need to go to that will be hard, I plan to do only that for the day. I bring friends when I can. This also applies to people. If someone feels draining, step back. Your energy supply is going to be drastically reduced from before. Focus on what is important. Focus on what will take care of your children (and you) the most.

Here is what I wrote on this subject. It is a lot of letting go of who you were in the world and finding a new place. It might be fragile and scary, but it's new footing.

I cannot support you. (Even though I want to.)
I will not hold you up. (Even though I want to.)
I cannot handle your pain too. (Even though I want to.)
Do not rely on me. (Even though you used to.)
Do not count on me. (Even though there was
time you could.)
Do not expect that even what I say I will do will get done.
(I don't have the memory anymore.)
Expect silence (because I cannot afford to talk).
No I am not over it (not even close).
No I don't even know how to move on (not that I want to).
No I am not happy. (I have you fooled though, haven't I?)
No, my world is not the same; it is unrecognizable to my
own eyes. It is void of what made it my home, my family,
my life. Home is where my Ollie is. So, no. I have no home.

One of the best things I did for myself was to find a supportive, caring, nurturing counselor. I went once a week. I still go once a week. My first experience with a counselor after Ollie died was the wrong fit, to say the least. I felt he was leading me in what I was supposed to be feeling and diagnosing me before we knew each other. I even corrected him at one point when he told me what I was experiencing, and he said that if I wasn't having nightmares yet, that I would. He made me uncomfortable, implied more than once that I would have to pay and that I had or would have PTSD symptoms. It was bad. It was off-putting at a time when I was still in shock and feeling like maybe I didn't need to have counseling. If you run into a bad fit, don't go back; just look for a new one. If they talk about the five stages of grief like they are linear and as if you will work through grief and be done someday, leave. The stages are cyclical. You go around and around in them in all different orders and patterns. Grief, my friend, is never done. It becomes a part of us. It is love. When I found my counselor, she felt like an older, wiser friend who listened and gave feedback when I needed it. Wherever I was at was okay and normal. She talks about supporting myself and building my life in a new way that incorporates my past. Having an hour in your week when you are forced to process in a safe place is self-care. Do it.

Your sexual desire might not die with your spouse. This does not mean you do not miss or love your significant other, but sometimes downstairs does not get the idea that your partner is dead. So go and buy an adult toy. It is okay to grieve while taking care of your physical need. The first dozen orgasms I had I emotionally fell apart afterward because the brain and the body are not always in alignment. It is okay to have sexual needs even in grief and it is okay to cry afterward.

Life after your spouse dies can feel very difficult. I just wrote that sentence and thought about how dumb that sounds. Of course it's hard. Your world will never be the same and yet everything you have to do from day to day is still the same. I want you to know that after death, going to the bank can feel hard. Getting the mail can feel hard. And something can feel hard one day and the next day be nothing. *Anything* can feel hard. Seeing his toothbrush in the toothbrush holder can feel hard. Throwing it away can feel impossible. I call these little deaths.

little deaths
his deodorant died today
the one that had his DNA

It was gone as was he
the last milk he drank from the carton
the last pillowcase his head ever touched...
the last cell that he kissed floats to the ground from my lips
Death after Death after Death
each taking a piece of me.
Chipped away by all of the
little deaths

Be easy with yourself. Acknowledge where you are and what is hard. Do what you can and don't do anything you are not ready to do. The toothbrush can stay where it is for as long as you want it there.

There is moving forward with life and doing things that feel hard. It will feel uncomfortable. If you have a moment where something feels possible (like going to your first wedding solo), step out of your comfort zone, say yes, but have an exit plan. My first experience doing this was a child's birthday party. I knew my son would feel left out if we did not go. I wanted him to feel normal. So we went. It was not easy. It felt uncomfortable and hard even though I knew most of the people there. In the beginning, just the fact that everyone else's life was fully intact felt impossibly hard. My children played and smiled and laughed and I held on to that.

We were at a party last night. There were so many families and kids and so much laughter and running. Louis was on the trampoline, and he was so beautiful and adorable. I was laughing at the joy he had while jumping and playing and falling. I looked around to share that moment with someone. Anyone. See my baby boy with me. Please! I need to share this with someone! The ache of loss for the father of that baby was so profound and large and bottomless at that moment. I wanted to witness someone's joy from watching Louis. I wanted to watch his joy from watching Louis.

A nine-year-old girl rescued me. She came and watched and felt love and joy for the dancing eighteen-month-old on the trampoline.

Stretch yourself when you can. Stretch yourself and then reflect. Stretch yourself but have your excuse ready to leave. Have your exit strategy. An exit strategy can be anything from, "I'm feeling a little ill" to, "We have another engagement in twenty minutes" to, "I just can't take any more." Use your exit strategy when you have to.

Choose small joy and look for your wins. From the day Ollie died I decided to look for the beautiful things.

I chose to experience awe and wonder. I chose to keep my heart open to good and beauty. Friend, it is a choice and a choice you need to make.

I walked out of the hospital on the third day in May and faced toward the east, above the parking lot, above the death of my Ollie. There were the mountains, tall and still and majestic. Above them was a blue sky with white billowy clouds.

I think about leaving this place a lot. I think of the work that comes with New England winters, and then I look up. All directions, all seasons, I see the beauty of this land and all of those mountains. The same mountains that spoke to me and said, "There is more than this. We are bigger than this ..."

I take pictures of nature and people and things I love. I write about moments that I don't want to forget. I listen to the wind chimes. I stop to smell the lily of the valley. I enjoy the cheesecake. I mean, I close my eyes and *enjoy* the cheesecake. I talk about Ollie. A lot. I tell our funny stories and watch people laugh. I laugh if I find something funny, even when others don't. I light candles and get soft rugs that, when I put my feet on them, feel so good. I get a babysitter and go out with my friends.

I dance. I sing. I go down the slip and slide and roller coasters with my kids. I paint my nails glittery bright colors so that when I look at my hands I don't see the missing ring; I see the sparkles.

Do what connects you to beauty and joy. Do what makes you laugh and smile. Do what connects you to this life again. Do it. Whatever it is. Find it and do it.

I look for the good, and I give credit. I look for the good even if it is as small as "I put deodorant on this morning," "I took my three-year-old to school" (I might have been fifty minutes late, but he got there), "I have made it to month three." Some days your successes will be major. Other times they will be little. Just acknowledge them. You did it. You made it one more day. I know I'm proud of you.

Certain days and times will be worse. For me, bedtime and weekends are hard. Ollie did bedtime. The kids listened to Ollie. They don't listen to me. They fight and talk over my reading. They wait until I threaten to get their pajamas on. It is hard. Weekends feel never-ending. There is no routine to fall back on, and there is almost always something we are doing that makes me feel stretched. Ollie was always home on weekends.

Things to Try for Your Tough Days and Times

Routine

Every bedtime works in the same way. The kids know the routine and so do I. I can count down the steps.

For weekends, I use the one-event-a-day rule. I do one thing a day: one party, one park, one activity.

I also try to keep bedtime consistent so that I know my day with kids ends at 7:30. You know that you are off duty after bedtime, and there are some days where that is what will keep you going. Knowing exactly when it is going to end can be a relief. You need boundaries to remain healthy. I do enough that the kids remain connected and happy, but I do not overdo activities.

Plan for the crap days

Plan for the days you do not have the will to do much at all. If you don't let your kids watch TV, have a movie day. If you don't usually play with Play-Doh, drop it on the table. Keep some things special so that when you have nothing left you have a way to get a break. This is also the time to call your tribe. There is nothing like a friend showing up and sitting with you—

and if they have kids, your kids have a new distraction. There have been many days when I call a friend to come over and order pizza, and if one can't come, I invite the next. Have your bag of tricks that are special enough to give you a break.

Chapter 8:

STEP 5 - HOW TO SUPPORT YOUR CHILDREN IN GRIEF

I get up in the morning. I put on clothes. I brush my teeth. I feed my children. I take them to school. I pick them up. I feed them again. I put them to bed. I take them to birthday parties, play dates, museums, parades. … I shield them, by doing all this "normal." There are so many days I do not want to get up. I want to severely grieve. I do not have that luxury because I have to function, for my children.

I know how important your children are. They are why you are trying so hard. They are your link to your spouse. They are what is good and hard. You want to make sure they are okay. You want to make sure that no matter what you have been handed, they will grow up stable, healthy, and happy. This is my advice for parenting in grief.

Be honest with your children. When I am really sad, I tell them. When they ask something about Ollie's death, I tell them at an age-appropriate level. For Teddie, my three-year-old, I tell him Mommy misses Daddo and that is why she is sad. With Oscar, five years old, I might say that I saw a picture of Daddo cooking and when I looked at the stove it reminded Mommy that Daddo was dead and I miss him. With Louis, the one-year-old, Mommy is sad. When I am irrationally angry, I tell them. I include them in my process. Oscar knows that his Daddo died of asphyxiation, which is not being able to breathe. He knows the car fell on his dad when he was working on it. He asked to see the pictures taken after Ollie died, and I showed him. I want them to know what is happening with me, and I want them to know that I will answer their questions.

Children process differently. They will be sad for five minutes and then be back to playing. Grief can also come out as anger and anxiety. Anxiety in children can show up as being afraid of the dark, having separation anxiety, or not wanting to participate in things that they used to want to do. It could come out as not liking feeling out of control. Oscar was in the car the other day and said, "Mom, I am not going to fix cars." I said, "Okay, baby." He said, "I don't want to die like Daddo." That same week I was zip-tying the a plastic piece until it could get fixed on the van and Oscar came out and said, "Are you fixing the car?" I had to explain how I was not under the car and that I was very safe where I was. The first time I left Oscar, my parenting expert told me to write him notes and send pictures of me throughout the day because you cannot convince a child who has lost a parent that you are going to come back. Children have fewer words and less self-awareness to be clear where feelings are coming from. Being aware and meeting these outbursts with love and compassion instead of punishment can go a long way. Also giving words to feelings when they appear gives your child a vocabulary for what is happening.

Show them your grieving process. I cry puddled on the floor in front of my children. I hold them when they let me. I tell them how much their Daddo loved them and how sad I am that he is not here to tell them himself. I tell them how much they look like him. I take them outside to scream with me. I burn messages with them. We sing happy birthday to Daddo as I cry. I tell them stories and cry. I take them when I scatter ashes. We talk about Ollie's life and death. We talk about how sad Mommy is. Now if I cry, they ask if I am missing Daddo.

If you are like me, you will sometimes feel like a failure. I say often that I was a better mother before Ollie died. I had so much more patience. I didn't raise my voice as often. I was calm. The first year, I yelled a lot. My voice would be sore because I yelled all day. I decided not to yell one day. The boys had dragged a ton of toys into my room and I asked a good seven times for them to pick them up. Oscar finally responded by taking his guitar, standing it up on my bed, and saying, "I like it here." I whispered, "Oscar, watch this." And I took the guitar and stomped on it with my bare foot.

I don't always win at adulting. At my first Camp Widow, I was in a parenting workshop and the thing that stuck with me was that the presenter said, "I yelled so much. I yelled that whole year. And you know what? My kids are fine. They are productive, happy young adults." So I am going to say the same to you. Your children are going to be fine. They are going to be fine because they have a kick-butt parent who loves them so much as to work on herself in the worst time of her life. They have you.

Keep living. Make new memories. I am a solo parent with three kids. We still go places. I still put my kids in a car and drive fifteen hours to places by myself. We go to amusement parks, museums, and pools. We make new memories, take new pictures, and have new firsts. These trips are not vacations for me. I actually call them trips. They are work. They are hard work, but I want my children to know that we still live. The first trip that we took was a month after Ollie passed. We were meeting my parents, but I was driving by myself. I remember the anxiety I had taking all my kids into a rest area that had tons of people. I remember the feeling of betrayal that Ollie was not there with me. I remember getting one look from someone and feeling like I wanted to scream that my husband was dead and that was why I had three boys by myself in a rest area.

It was hard the first time. It was slightly easier the next time. You adjust. You get better. Then, when your three-year-old talks about the ride he went on at Busch Gardens, you know you did it for a good reason. I look at pictures of our travels and adventures and feel proud of myself. I feel like Ollie would approve. I feel a sense of accomplishment. They make me happy. I also ask if anyone wants to go with us. Anywhere. My girlfriend and I just took our five children to the beach in Maine by ourselves. What is great is we laughed the entire time. There is video of us just living the experience of trips with children. The boys peeing in empty water bottles, the meltdowns, the chasing children in the water so they don't get swept away. I laugh every time I watch them. I laugh and think, that was worth it. They will remember that and so will I. Just a general tip: get a house or a first-floor condo if you're traveling with five children. You can thank me later.

I feel it is my job to keep Ollie alive for the children. We watch videos of their dad. When we eat cherries, I talk about how much he loved cherries. When they do something exactly like their dad did, I tell them. If we go to places that remind me of their father, I share that. I have other people talk about Ollie. At the funeral I had people write memories of Ollie. I keep in touch with Ollie's family and friends so my children will have their stories. I know that my younger children are highly unlikely to have any memory of Ollie on their own, but I want them to have what I can give them. This is the saddest part of losing Ollie for me. I wish my children had been older and had more time and memories of him.

Ollie use to make up silly songs and every now and then they pop back into my mind. Every night Ollie would put the kids to bed and my oldest would say, "I love Mama, Teddie, and Louie." Ollie would say, "I love Mama, Teddie, and Louie too." Oscar would say, "Guess what? I love you." And Ollie would say, "I love you too." Oscar would say, "Night night." Ollie, "Night night." Oscar, "Kiss kiss." Ollie, "Kiss kiss," and then he would kiss him and repeat the whole thing with the next child. We do this every night. What is nice about keeping Ollie alive for the boys is that he stays alive in me.

Books have been a lifesaver for me and for the kids. There are some amazing authors who have put words to grief in such simple terms for children. *The Invisible String* by Patrice Karst, *The Goodbye Book* by Todd Parr, and many others are so lovingly written to describe such big feelings to such small and tender beings. I remember reading the last page of *The Goodbye Book*: "We all get sad when we say goodbye to someone we love. Always try to remember the happy times you shared together. The end. Love, Todd." My brother was there and we just bawled together.

Some books for children I have appreciated are

- *The Invisible String* by Patrice Karst, illustrated by Geoff Stevenson
- *Something Very Sad Happened: A Toddler's Guide to Understanding Death* by Bonnie Zucker, illustrated by Kim Fleming
- *The Goodbye Book* by Todd Parr
- *Where Do They Go?* by Julia Alvarez, illustrated by Sabra Field
- *The Feelings Book* by Todd Parr (not specifically related to death but great when trying to help your child put words to feelings)

Counseling is as important for children as adults. There are so many incredible play-based therapists who can guide your children through their feelings. It gives them space to process with someone who is specifically trained to help children. Take advantage of their knowledge.

I know I am a better mother when I get breaks. When I do not get breaks, I yell a lot. I sometimes feel so angry and desperate that I lock myself in my room for a couple of minutes so that I don't do something I regret.

My youngest, Louie, was one when Ollie died. He is now two and a half. I put him in childcare. I put him in childcare because I need some time when I am not the one responsible. I need to go to doctors' appointments by myself. I need a break. I need a nap.

Support yourself with childcare. You need a moment to be an adult and you are missing the other half who gave you time. Your kids will be okay. You are still a good parent. You have to take care of yourself so you can take care of them. The same goes for nights out. You need space to miss your children. Take it.

Chapter 9:

STEP 6 - TAKING CARE OF YOUR HEART

There are many days when the idea of waking up again will feel painful, sometimes almost impossible. These are the days you will need a toolbox of things to make living just even an ounce more worth doing. Your heart is broken and there is nothing to repair it, nor is there anything to fill that gaping hole. So what can you do? All of this list can be used to connect you to your higher source or all living things—whatever you feel called to. Life force that runs through us and this world is what we have to seek out. *Seek it out.* We have to be even more vigilant to find beauty, joy, and peace because they can be so lost under the fog of grief. Here is my short list to reconnect you to all that is, when life can feel so consumed by grief.

1. Create a playlist. From months three through seven, I set my alarm to Andra Day singing "Rise Up." At this time my four-year-old always ended up in bed with me so the song would come on, I would look at Teddie (who had usually been up for at least forty minutes), and we would sing it to each other. Teddie is not my best speaker and his half-pronounced words always made me smile. I feel Ollie's presence when the boys make me smile. I listen almost every night while I am in the shower to "Georgica Pond" by Johnnyswim. It was sung at both of Ollie's funerals and was a song and a group that make me feel close to him. In the car, I have the list of songs that meet me where I am at on a given day. Lately it has been "100 Bad Days" by AJR, "Won't Back Down" by Tom Petty, "Confident" by Demi Lovato, "Truth Hurts" by Lizzo, and "Live While We're Young" by Johnnyswim. They sometimes make perfect sense and sometimes they

don't. Either way, if you feel better listening to them, do it.

2. One of the biggest conduits of my grief and recovery is writing (surprise, right?). A month after Ollie died, I took the writing your grief course with Megan Devine. Megan has a course where you get a prompt a day to write your inner emotions and what is in your heart. Most of the writings from my first year were yielded from the prompts and they paint a beautiful picture of grief for my children if they ever want to experience it through my thoughts. It was profoundly impactful in my processing and grieving the beautiful man who left this earth trapped under a van.

This was my first journal entry:

I am not the person I used to be ... I am fragile and resilient. I have inner strength that I never knew I had to do things I never wanted or intended to do. All of that and my soul is paper thin. One comment, thought, or problem can cut deep and I bleed out onto the floor.

I am not the person anymore that thought I had control. My thoughts make my reality. I did not think up this garbage. I am not the person who skimmed the surface. I am in the depth of pain and mourning that covers my life and me. I have learned what is more precious than gold. I am not a lover anymore. My bed lies empty from across the room.

My heart has expanded to love the intangible and contracted to cry myself to sleep. My mind leaves most things to the side so it can vigorously work on putting the pieces of loss and continuance together. No. I am not the person I used to be and I never will be again

Journal, write poetry, write about your feelings or the world or how angry you are. Write about your love. The life you could have had, and the life you now want to create. Write like your soul depends on it. Write like your heart will feel so much more and so much less at the same time. Write for your heart.

On grief: I am the longing for what once was. I am the echo of a past that cannot be forgotten. I am the future that will never be. I am the knot in your stomach and the lump in your throat. I am the wound that will never heal.

I am constant and consuming. I bring depth to the shallow. I bring conflict to the peaceful. I am ever lurking in the background, waiting for stillness, or triggers. I am waiting for you to feel overwhelmed or lonely. I am waiting for you to feel happy or proud.

I mean no harm. I am the byproduct of love freely given. I am the reminder of the unknown and the reminder of where all things go on this earth. Ashes to ashes. Dust to dust. Life is for the living and I am for those who have lived longer.

Two things that have really helped me are creating a bucket list and asking myself whether the eighty-five-year-old Charity would say yes or no. Let me tell you, eighty-five-year-old Charity is a force to be reckoned with. She really would do almost anything. I think these tools give you things to do still. For many, many months and honestly moments now, I have just wanted to be with him. If it was as easy as lying down and never getting back up again, I would have been all for it. But these strategies give you things to do and accomplish before you leave this earth. My first my bucket list item was to take the kids to Disney. Why Disney? Because Ollie absolutely did not want to go. So I lovingly refer to it as the "eff you for dying, I'm going to Disney" trip, FYF-DIGTDT for short. Other things on my list? Live in a different country, do stand-up comedy, be in better shape than I have ever been in my life, sing a solo, go sailing. The biggest is to create a legacy by impacting people's lives and loving people wholeheartedly and doggedly. There are so many more. I want to feel alive. I want to feel like, if I go tomorrow, whoever is telling my story will say, "She was a bada** with a nice a**."

Get out of town. Get out of town with your kids, like we talked about before, but also get out of town without your children. Live an adult life even for that brief weekend (or, if you get really lucky and have excellent friends and family, whole week). Recharge your battery. I went away to Camp Widow in Toronto. I also went to visit my friend who I met at Camp Widow in Montreal, where she lives, for our birthday weekend. We went to the art museum, and she mentioned how quiet I was. It was because I had not been that quiet in years. I just got to look at art and enjoy the beauty around me without worrying what my kid might knock down or when they would complain about being hungry. We also went to nice restaurants and a Swedish spa (where there was no talking!!!) and just got to be together as adults. These moments of adulthood are critical. I always say I am a better mother when I get a moment to miss them.

Learn from experts. I took that writing course. I also was feeling like the most out of control, crappy parent on the face of the earth, so I hired a parenting expert who I would talk to once a week about how I was coping. This was one of the best decisions I ever made. I could easily text her to get advice on how each individual child was acting. I felt empowered instead of scared and alone, and I had someone to bounce ideas off. She also had me write a parenting manifesto so that I had a tool to look at when I felt conflicted about what I should be doing at a given time. Are my actions leading to the grown men I wanted to create? I also took a spiritual course in order to try to reconnect with my inner voice because I felt so shut off emotionally and spiritually. I went to a healer. I still go to counseling once a week. If you are looking for answers, look for people who really will have them. Outside experts will not have the "I am judging you" vibe and if they do, get a new expert.

I am writing this, and as I type, I hate it as much as I believe it is absolutely critical. You absolutely have to make new positive life-affirming memories. I'm not just talking about with your children. If you got eaten up in wife and motherdom, it is time to find your adult. The first trip I took alone was for a night to Mirror Lake Inn in Lake Placid, New York. I was all by myself, and I thought that I needed some space to mourn. I booked a couple of services at the spa and had a really nice meal at the restaurant and consumed a champagne flight. I sat alone feeling awkward and lost without Ollie, but when I got up to the room, half drunk, I was so not used to drinking I fell asleep at 8:30. I woke up at 4:00 a.m. and took a bath because I was not used to sleeping. The next morning I booked it back to the kids because I was so bad at being alone. The moral of this sad story is that you cannot force mourning to be on your timeframe, and starting out on new journeys is hard. I now can sit and have dinner alone and love every moment of the quiet. I can taste the food, eavesdrop on everyone's conversations, and be quiet and alone well and naturally.

In terms of making new memories, I go somewhere every two months by myself or with friends. I went with a group of women to an ice bar for a weekend. We all packed into one suite and bundled up and laughed our way through the weekend. Why? I need to feel human and alive. I need to create new memories with new adults who make me smile and laugh. Throughout these adventures I always take Ollie with me. I talk about him, I share inside jokes, and I remember him while living. I take him with me. Just last week I went to Jamaica for a week with a friend. There are always moments when it hits you like a ton of bricks that you miss your spouse, when the friend says or does something that would have been different. But there are the moments that you look at the beauty around you and you realize that even if we all become particles once more, little cells and pieces of cosmic dust, we are of this world and this world is amazing. Ollie is the ocean and sand, the waves, and the air. We return to the earth at least physically, and I feel Ollie while looking at beauty. Always.

Express yourself, even if you feel you aren't "good" at it. Artistic expression gives a glimpse of light in the darkness. It can be photography, writing, dancing—whatever feels healing or will let you believe there is something beautiful in the world. Take a class, take pictures with your phone, do whatever lightens your space, even if only for a minute.

Looking at my Instagram from last year is like taking a trip down "looking for the good" lane. It brings back the uncertainty and the hope. The hope that if I can see that flower now, I will see the bigger picture of joy and peace later on.

Listen or read (if you can) other people's stories and advice. This was another way to get closer to the community I had unwillingly joined. It gave voice to expressions and ideas I had no time to form. It is a very active way to process.

I didn't know that it would just spill out like vomit on the page. There were some days that I just thought, "I am too tired, I can't think." When I would finally open the prompt and sit down at the computer, my words came spilling fast and harsh against the page. I wrote for others about Ollie. I wrote his eulogy. I wrote informing people. I wrote to explain who he was to me. This was the first time I wrote for myself. Nothing that is pretty or blunted. This is raw and open and wounded and hard to read, and beautiful. I didn't know how much I censored myself.

I really enjoy death jokes. I just recently told someone that they were not allowed to die in the pool because two deaths on my property would look suspicious. I told my Christian book study that Ollie and I thought we needed to have a baby in October because we would then have a birthday every month from September to February. I explained that instead of having a baby in October, we just got rid of September. At Christmas time I was texting a friend and she suggested I get a washer tub to put under a live tree because when they begin to die, they make a huge mess. I replied that Ollie already did that to the driveway so I think once is enough. I have always used humor, but for some reason it feels like I take my story back when I do this. I take some of the control that I totally never had back. I feel maybe this would all be more common if death was not so feared and treated as an actual part of life. It is, you know. It is life.

Life is for the living and grief is for those who live longer.

Get out and do something physical. Dance. God, dance is good for the soul. Sad dance, happy dance, just move your body. Feel the beat or the words—just move. Walk, run, punch (my favorite), or kick. Let your body produce its natural endorphins and feel the joy of your body being able (in whatever way it can be). Seriously, kick the soccer ball hard. *It does not matter how far the ball goes.* Kick it again. Hit stuff. Smash stuff. Swim. Get out and sweat and hurt. I went to CrossFit to literally hurt so much I could not think about Ollie, to make me hurt so much I cannot think of anything but what I am doing. Climb the mountain, ski, mountain bike. I have actually used my lack of fear about death to do things that I never thought I would. I was horseback riding, and the guy said, "Are you ready for some jumps?" I said, "Heck, yes" before I realized he was joking. He told me that was not the answer he was expecting. I feel like this lack of fear is a gift. I am not scared of things that used to terrify me. I embrace the pain and adrenaline. Get lost? What does that matter? Have a bad interaction? Who cares? Get out there. *Do* the stuff you want to do but used to be afraid of.

Chapter 10:

STEP 7 - CONNECTING TO SPIRIT

I n essence, this is what, when all else fails, keeps you afloat. I know that many times, feeling connected to a higher source when your world looks like it has been burned to the ground by that same higher source is a hard pill to swallow—a really hard pill. After Ollie passed, I fluctuated between feeling extremely connected and so distant that it felt hard to breathe. I am not here to advocate for a specific faith system. I myself have a Christian background but have not felt that as a title that I can hold to for a long time. My advice in this is to listen to your soul. Listen to your inner guidance and what it is telling you.

If it helps, do it. I do a lot of things that might be considered weird. I hold Ollie's hand in the car when there is no one sitting in the passenger seat. I talk aloud to him all of the time, I listen for messages through songs played on the radio, lights turning on and off and flickering, through orbs in photos, and my right face and arm feeling warm and tingly. When I was having the breakup talk (which was good for both of us) with one of the first guys I dated after Ollie died, there was a good sixty-second pause, and then Alexa said, "Here is a song I think you will enjoy"—and it was "Blame It on Me" by George Ezra. I looked at the now-ex boyfriend and said, "That's my husband."

Ollie bought me a weighted blanket for our anniversary, a month before his passing. It was supposed to help with my night terrors (it did seem to keep me in bed more) but the night terrors persisted as normal.

I started having night terrors when I was twenty-four, the year I met Ollie. He has lived with me sitting and screaming every night (sometimes multiple times) for the fifteen years we were together. One thing I would cry out was, "Mommy."

On the day he died, I screamed and I cried out, "Mommy."

I have not had a night terror since.

I also think the only reason I have been able to fall asleep is because of that weighted blanket.

My shower door opens almost every time I take a shower. The light in the children's room turns red, the color that Ollie would always turn it on. I use a medium. I light candles, I wear Ollie's wedding ring. I do what I feel connects me to him and the divine. I put crystals in my pillow. I go to church. I sing. Whatever connects you to your source, do it. Walk on the earth without shoes, go to a sweat lodge liturgical dance, follow the moon cycles, celebrate El Día de Los Muertos. Spread ashes, go to favorite spots. I lie in the spot where Ollie died. I lie there just to be in the place where he last breathed. I lie there and cry.

I go to church again.
I go because it is the same as when I was a child.

It is one thing that you, my love, were never a part of.
I close my eyes and listen to the cadence of voices speaking.
I close my eyes and listen to the rhythmic singing.
I sit alone in stillness and breath.
I feel no draw to the message, or to the God that they speak of in this place.
My God lives in no building.
My God cannot be put to words.
Yet I sit. I sit and fall away from the world into the embrace of ritual.

On the flip side, if it doesn't feel right, don't do it. If you think that you should be going to church every week and it makes you feel like crap, stop. If you don't want to put his ashes where everyone else does, don't. If someone tells you that dead people come back as butterflies and you think that is total crap, don't believe it. Don't get stuck in anything. Use what works and get rid of what doesn't. Seriously, who knew your loved one more than you? No one.

This also feels counterintuitive, especially in the beginning. I know I still have huge urges to just want to be with Ollie. I don't want to live anymore. If an asteroid hit the earth at those exact moments, my last second would be spent saying, "Bring it on," but when there is something beautiful or worth celebrating, celebrate it. The first time I stepped back into the hospital that Ollie died in, it was because my good friends had had a beautiful baby girl a month after Ollie died. I chose to celebrate Meredith and my friends by walking into that building. I chose to love them more than my hate for the location. We have birthday parties. We celebrate Ollie's birthday. Why? *Because you are still alive.* You are still alive. Feel alive. As I said, I am preparing to do things I would never have done. Skydiving, getting a tattoo, running a marathon. Why? Because I can. Ollie cannot. I can. I want my children to look at my life and say, "She was a warrior." As I mentioned before, I ask if my eighty-five-year-old self would say yes or no to an opportunity. My eighty-five-year-old self says yes.

He died. It opened a chasm of sorrow that would expand and contract at will, leaving her gasping for breath for years to come. Life never revealed any, "This is why, and you are better for it." Because there is no why.

The idea that I am better because of this death takes away my power. Any better that I am is because I have fought through the effects of death. It is because I am determined to live for my children. It is because I am determined to eventually say I want to live for myself. There is no redemption from Ollie because redemption implies rising up from something that is worse. He was always better. He will always be better. Survival story? Yes. I hope to someday report, "And she found happiness again, still clinging to the things and people that made her. She survived and made gardens out of weeds and art out of garbage."

Love like it's your job. Love your neighbor, love yourself, love your enemies, love those who don't understand you. Love those who use you. Love those who love you. Love hard. Love harder than you ever have. Open your eyes to what people are really showing you. See the brokenness and beauty of everyone. Love the earth and the heavens. Look around and find something to love. There was a quote going around Facebook about a wife saying to her husband to take the love he had for her and spread it to the world. No matter if there is anything after this (and I believe there is), use this time to love. Use this time to leave an indelible mark on as many souls and plants and places as you can. Love like it is your job. Surprise people with how much you love them. Show people what unconditional love is. While you are in love, there is less room for despair.

Home will find you. Ollie died and I felt like I lost my home. I had no footing. Home will come back. It won't look like what you had or what you wanted, but the people who love you will build it for you. I have been on a week's trip and on the airplane flying home and all I've been able to say is, "I want to go home to my children, and friends." I want to hug and kiss my newly built family, I want to see them and listen to all that has happened. I want to swim and laugh and eat with them. They are my people. They are my soul mates and I love them like they were blood.

Find the beauty in the middle of hurt. Choose to see your children's smiles and hear their laughter and let it spark your heart. Choose to know that there is better even in the darkness of now. Fight for your life.

When she laughs, it's like a ray of sunshine that has been the only light to a dark room. Her arms are solace with the warmth that surrounds her. I think, I think it is love. When do you recover from catastrophe? Maybe never, but her face says there is something worthy of living longer ... even when she cannot see it.

Get quiet. I hardly watch TV anymore. I crave my time alone after the children go to bed. You need time to think and breathe. Again, I am not at the place where I can fully meditate, but I can count my breaths and I can listen to the shower. Sometimes quietness and stillness are when we can feel our loved ones the most. Sometimes it is just a gift to be still. Enjoy the quiet.

Find comfort in what you believe. If you believe your loved one is in heaven, I 100 percent support that. I believe that when we die we return to Source (God), and we decide if we need to learn more, which is when we return to different lives. I believe we make soul contracts with those who play important roles in our lives. This is comforting to me because I believe it is all now, the present moment, there is no past or future and what I am experiencing is a blip on the radar of time. Before I know it I will be one with everything again, including Ollie. Ollie and I (and you, for that matter) are all one, playing the idea of separateness. So when I feel alone, I open to the idea that it is me separating myself from all that is. Source meets us when we open to it and I am source and Ollie is source. Use your resources, your prayers, your studying to support your journey, and as I said before, if it doesn't fit anymore, get rid of it.

There are moments I feel a great peace in the present. When I feel connected to all that is. I am a part of the vast whole of the universe, where nothing can be separated. In those moments, I feel close to him, and I feel this path is possible. It is like a switch in the brain. ON: "I have lost nothing, because all is you and now." OFF: "He has died. I am alone without my partner." ON: "heart open." OFF: "heart broken."

The word softer has been with me this month, and I think I would benefit from everything being just a little bit softer; softer to process, softer to transition, softer to hold. Softer gives me breathing space. Softer also means thinking of him less. It means being in the moment more. Softer means letting go a little bit more. Softer is being present now. I know Ollie would want softer for me. Easier said than done.

Chapter 11:

WHY SHOULD I TRY?

So we are here. I have given you advice. You are now thinking, "Is this feel-good crap or something I really should invest my time (which I have none) and effort (which standing up takes effort) into? Should I try? Because I really don't want to." There are days that I don't want to either. At all. Giving up is not an option. What is the reason that doesn't work so well? I have these babies who I want to be well and happy. I want them to see their mommy yank herself out of the harsh horrible reality that has been put in front of her and make a life to be proud of. Ollie's grandmother lost her husband when her youngest was in high school. She sold his businesses, invested, and worked part-time at a doctor's office for a very long time. She had a twenty-five-year-old live with her for a year, she had a married pilot who flew her around to different countries, and in the end she had a loving boyfriend whom she would not marry because I don't think she wanted to take care of another man. She threw parties, she did continuing education, she watched her great-grandchildren, and she traveled. She lived through her husband's death and the deaths of two of her four children. She was a powerful, resourceful woman. And so are you. You would not have picked up this book if you were not a proactive, "I want to do the best for me and my children" kind of person. There is no way you would be reading these words if not. So props. You have already taken a gigantic step, and it isn't reading this book. It is caring enough to try.

I guess my thought on the whole matter is, there is strength in numbers. You need a tribe, and I want to be part of that. When you need a reminder to step back and love yourself or believe the sign your spouse is giving you, I want you to have me at your back. Because that is exactly where I want to be. I've got your back. I've got you when you are on the floor and don't know how you will ever get up, and I've got you when you have your playlist on and you are actually feeling empowered and moving forward. I've got you. I know you. I am you, just slightly in the future. From where I sit, the first year for me was, "How do I do this?" I'm scared, I'm alone, every piece of advice I get is usually tainted by what that person wants or thinks I should do because they imagine grief to be linear and something you get over. That is not me, nor is it this book. I'm going to get you from A to B. My spouse died and I have small children, yet I am still alive and working toward a new normal at the end of year one. Year two is a whole new ball of wax, but you'll make it to year two. Which again makes you amazing in my book.

The other alternative can be devastating for your children and for yourself: if you give up now. (I'm not talking just about suicide, but again if that is even a notion, get help now.) Giving up can take so many forms (not getting up out of bed, not eating, eating too much, using ways to numb yourself, dropping into paralyzing despair). If any of these things happen, do one thing: get help.

If you give up now, your children have just lost both of their parents. If you give up now but decide to try later, you will be dealing with children who have grieved both parents and then have trust issues because one has suddenly tried to come back online. If you give in to grieving that looks like giving up, that is what your children are learning: give up when things are hard and awful.

Ladies and gentlemen, this is life on earth. There will be some point where things get rough and awful. But you will make it to year two. You will just have to do all the work then; because with grief, you have to do the work. I'm here for you. I've got your back. I know you don't want to, but you are going to because that is who you are.

Chapter 12:

HOME - IT'S TIME TO BUILD A NEW ONE

I thought to myself, that is exactly what I lost the day Ollie died. Home. The place to land no matter what falls apart. I thought of all my dear friends here who put shelter around the homeless soul and piece-by-piece widened their homes to cover us. How beautiful and such a gift that our homes are so expandable and adaptable to cover those we love even before they know that new home is being lovingly crafted for them.

The awful news is your life is in pieces. Nothing will ever be the same and you will always get to play the "what if they lived" game. The good news is that every little effort you make is building momentum for creating a life worth living. Not what you wanted, but a life that has beauty and joy and love. This book gives you the baby steps to build a foundation on. It gives you the ability to say, "At least I wrote down that feeling today. At least I knew to give myself some slack and remember I am going to have the days that I can't adult." It gives you the knowledge and the tools to know that you are normal and that you can do something small when your energy is at its lowest.

Your tribe will help you with this. They will send you texts and answer their phones. Even when your in-person tribe don't, your online tribe will. If you use this book as your guide and step up and step out, even baby steps, a new life, a new home will start building around you. No, it won't bring them back or be "better" than what you lost. It doesn't work like that. You have to choose to see the light, and the beautiful thing is, my babies create the most light for me. They are funny and wonderful and joyful. I can choose to see this. I can choose to be a part of it. You can too. Take it step by step, get the initial stuff done, learn what grief looks like, support yourself in daily living, find your tribe, take care of your children, open your heart, connect to spirit, and build your home brick-by-brick. It won't be easy, but the satisfaction of knowing where you came from and what you did will fill you with gratitude. At least, it did with me. We have to learn to find joy and peace in the now. If we are looking to be happy in the future when we find a new partner, get out of the house, find more friends, find better childcare, whatever it is, we are giving away our chance at peace and joy in the present moment, and all that we have is the present moment. We know all too well that we do not have the past and we also know that the future is not ours either. We have to build our house where we are right now. We have to find the beauty right now. We have to live as if our lives are worthy and worth living right now. We need to gather our tools and use them to remind us of our inner flames of unconditional love right now. Be present. Take action. The law of motion tells us things in motion stay in motion while things that are stopped stay stopped. You do you. Find your new self and strive to find meaning in this existence. You can do it. I know you can, because I did.

Kintsugi is the art of repairing pottery by using precious metals. It makes beautiful pieces of art and it makes the vessel stronger than it was originally. You, my friend, are brokenly beautiful. Repairing yourself. Making yourself stronger. Though you might not feel it or know it now, it is making you more beautiful, more true, more refined. That is gold you are filling your cracks and chips with. It is precious because it is coming from hard work and dedication to yourself and your children. You enter a holy place when you choose to repair instead of choosing to continue dysfunction. Your broken places will be filled with the beautiful love that has turned into grief because grief is love. My perspective on "important" and "relevant" has become so refined since Ollie died. I know what is important. I know what is not. I know that stuff does not matter and relationships and experiences do. I know this to my core. That is the stuff that is filling in your cracks, and it truly makes you a more beautiful person than so many because you see with eyes of experience—and experience is powerful. You get to impart life lessons to your children that others would not even have formed. Your children will learn to look for good, keep standing up when they fall, and openly love themselves and others because loss teaches us to love harder. Take what I have gathered and use it to love yourself harder. You've got this. I've got your back.

ACKNOWLEDGMENTS

To Laura, Lacey, Lyndsey, and Liz, thank you for holding me, especially in the days I could not stand by myself.

To Christine, Karrie, Teresa and Kate, thank you for your handholding and support exactly when I needed it.

To Ivy and Franz, thank you for holding down the fort while I poured my heart and soul into this book.

To my Mama, Daddy, Jayne, Scott, Debbie, Charlie, Rachelle, Sara, Ryan, and all of my family, your love envelops me every day.

To my boys, Oscar, Theodore, and Louis, who are the love that runs through my veins and the joy in every one of my smiles. I do it all for you.

And to my Ollie. Your love was the foundation I found the courage to build my true self on. You will forever be my hearts song calling to itself. My heart is now your home.

Thank you to Angela Lauria and The Author Incubator's team, as well as to David Hancock and the Morgan James Publishing team for helping me bring this book to print.

THANK YOU!

Thank you for trusting me! I hope that my journey and process have given you tools to find a softer way through the first couple of years without your loved one. I am amazed by you and so proud of your ability to seek help and advice through your grief. I hope that this book has truly become a survival guide for you as you seek to make a new home for yourself and your beautiful children.

I feel honored to be a part of your journey. I would love to continue on with you.

Visit my website, www.thewidowssurvivalguide.com, to schedule a complementary call for further support.

As always, I am here to hold your hand.

Love,

Charity

ABOUT THE AUTHOR

At thirty-seven, Charity woke up one morning as a wife and mother of three small boys and by noon was a widow and solo parent. In the first year of widowhood she created a successful business, raised three children, wrote a book, and became a coach to help others make it through in the worst time of their lives.

Her gentle heart, raw openness, and wit shine through in *The Widow's Survival Guide*.

Charity went from healer, to wife, to stay at home mother, to widow, to successful business owner, and back to healer and widow coach with her practical, loving survival guide for widows with children. Charity holds a BS and many certifications in the healing arts, which she uses to help widows and all who she coaches to find joy in the midst of chaos and grief. She lives with her three sons Oscar, Theodore, and Louis in rural Vermont. She honors her late husband Oliver by loving and serving others through her words and life work.